"In today's frenzied world, it's challenging to find stability for people to perform and maintain their well-being. Diane Allen has a wonderful approach to help everyone maneuver, adapt, and thrive. This resource can be applied to every employee at every level of an organization. I'm in !! Join the flow !!"

–Steve Browne, SHRM-SCP
Chief People Officer | LaRosa's, Inc.
Author of *HR on Purpose !!*, *HR Rising !!*
& *HR Unleashed !!*

"*Flow* is a masterclass for unlocking happiness, productivity, and so much more!"

–David Raymond
Psychology of Fun Expert, Original Phillie Phanatic

"Diane's flow strategic work is remarkable. As the CEO of a branding firm, I need our leadership team and employees to shift between creativity and logistics throughout the day. Diane's coaching with our team made this possible. I use Diane's technique numerous times every week in my work, and I know my employees do the same. I highly recommend her if you want a way for your team members to be able to access flow in their work more often."

–Chris West
CEO - Founder | Video Narrative Inc.

"Diane Allen's *Flow: Unlock Your Genius, Love What You Do* has shown me the incredible impact of being in a flow state. It's an essential tool for personal and professional growth, enabling employees to discover joy and fulfillment in their everyday tasks."

–Cindy Bene'
Author & HR Consultant | Employment Transition Solutions, LLC

"Diane Allen has captured in *Flow: Unlock Your Genius, Love What You Do,* the majestic power of "flow" that each of us has within us. She shares the simple steps of how to develop it to become the inspiring and motivating leaders that our teams and those around us need in their lives. This book will serve as a timeless and invaluable guide to create a workplace culture of the future where people can be fulfilled and live life to their full potential. I have personally come to see how being in your "flow state" impacts in dealing with stress and the interruptions life brings. This is a must-read for those who want to have those "magical moments where skills and passion align."

–Sue Falcone
Founder & CEO | Remarkable! A Speakers Bureau

"*Flow* brilliantly demystifies the concept of peak performance, making it accessible to all. Diane Allen's work is a must-read for anyone wanting to unlock their potential and create a more purposeful, joyful work life."

–Michael Harris
Business Coach, Yogi

"A truly transformative read! Whether you're leading yourself, a small team, or an entire organization, *Flow* by Diane Allen offers profound wisdom and practical strategies for you and your team to achieve sustained success and fulfillment. *Flow* provides the tools and inspiration for you to tap into your genius and live a life full of purpose and passion."

–Dr. Magie Cook
Motivational Speaker, Author, Entrepreneur

"Diane Allen's *Flow: Unlock Your Genius, Love What You Do* is an enlightening exploration of what it takes to be at our best—and the changes any of us can make to get there. With a straightforward narrative sprinkled with inspiring (and completely relatable) stories, readers will find step-by-step advice they can act on immediately. Whether you're trying to be a better leader or you're running into obstacles in your quest for excellence, *Flow* offers a practical and actionable approach to living your best life."

–Deb Trevino
Thought Leadership & Content Strategist

"In this welcome how-to manual on everything we need to know about flow, Allen makes concepts easy to absorb and apply. In a twist on a concept principally used for personal development, it's easy to see getting into the flow state as a vital productivity tool for leaders, teams, and individuals."

–Hayley Foster
Short Talk Expert for Over 1,000 Thought Leaders

"Diane's very personable writing style makes advanced psychological concepts more accessible to the layperson. She has clearly done "the work," and not only does she have the results to prove it, she is also helping others to achieve those results."

–Morgan Lane Bennett
Mindset & Executive Life Coach

"As someone who's performed and taught improv for decades, being in your flow state IS the state of mind that gives you access to everything you need to succeed: Deep listening, the ability to collaborate in any situation, and unlimited creativity. Diane's book *Flow* is such a pleasant read. I've seen Diane speak. She is relaxed, very honest, and very helpful. Reading *Flow* felt like Diane and I were sitting having coffee as she shared with me detailed recollections of her path to flow, and specific methods to get there on my own."

–John Breen
Founder | Bend Institute of Comedy,
Writer, Director, Business Consultant

"We all want more of what Diane has tapped into… flow! This book is a key for anyone who wants to unlock this magical state on demand for better (and happier) work and life."

–O'Brien McMahon
Senior Vice President | Lockton Companies, LLC

flow

Unlock Your Genius
Love What You Do

Diane Allen

Flow: Unlock Your Genius, Love What You Do
© 2024 by Diane Allen.

All rights reserved. No part of this publication may be reproduced, distributed, or transmitted in any form or by any means, including photocopying, recording, or other electronic or mechanical methods, without the prior written permission of the publisher, except in the case of brief quotations embodied in critical reviews and certain other noncommercial uses permitted by copyright law. For permission requests, email the author at diane@dianeallen.com

The advice provided by the author is based on personal and professional experience in dealing with issues surrounding flow; however, it is not a substitute for paid professional guidance. The studies and statistics quoted are, to the best of the author's knowledge and belief, accurate. This book is sold without warranties of any kind, express or implied, and both the author and publisher disclaim any liability, loss, or damage caused by its contents.

ISBN: 978-1-7378556-2-0 (Paperback)
ISBN: 978-1-7378556-3-7 (E-book)

Book design by Lieve Maas.

Printed in the United States of America
First printing edition 2024.

Incubation Press
Bend, OR

https://dianeallen.com

TABLE OF CONTENTS

Foreword   xi
by *Adam Nemer, Mental health leadership consultant*

Introduction   xv

CHAPTER 1: What's Possible?   1

CHAPTER 2: What is Flow?   19

CHAPTER 3: Discover Your Flow Strategy™   35

CHAPTER 4: Ignite Flow   63

CHAPTER 5: Lead with Flow   83

CHAPTER 6: Flow in Action   101

CHAPTER 7: In Flow   121

About the Author   129

FOREWORD

by *Adam Nemer, Leadership consultant and founder of Simple Mental Health*

Who would have thought that the single greatest executive coach and personal mental health advisor I ever worked with would be a concert violinist?

As a young man graduating from Claremont McKenna College in Southern California more than 30 years ago, I had one goal in life. Become self-actualized. I wanted to venture out and live a life where I could become the best possible version of myself.

Over the years, I worked hard at it. Really hard. I achieved a lot of traditional success—CFO of a multi-billion-dollar healthcare system; senior operations executive for a $4 ½-billion-dollar health plan. My children were thriving, and I actively participated in the community.

Yet, with hindsight, I was far from my dream of self-actualization. Something was missing. I chased one seeming priority after another. I got distracted by the tyranny of the urgent.

I wasn't happy.

And then, my life changed after a 45-minute chance encounter with Diane Allen in a coffee shop. We'd been attending the same conference but hadn't met.

We struck up a conversation in line while waiting for our drinks, and within a few minutes, Diane was holding an air violin and explaining the principles of flow.

Over the next half hour or so, she taught me how to do it. To get into flow. She walked me through the process with her trademark sage guidance and all the precision, care, and delicacy of a concert violinist.

She asked me the questions she poses for you here. In a single conversation, using the same exercise she shares with you here, Diane helped me realize what got me into flow.

It wasn't complicated for me. In fact, once I got there, it was easy. I just had to find the one trigger that got me into a state of Zen-like joy and productivity, where work was simply living.

For me, it's music. That's it. I start each day by pressing play and my flow begins. Like magic, that gets me into a state where I can be the best version of myself in the moment.

Now, as the founder of Simple Mental Health, like Diane, I help leaders create healthy cultures in their organizations by focusing on their own and their employees' mental well-being. And one of the very first questions I ask executives when I work with them is, "Do you know what gets *you* into flow?"

So, I want to ask you the same question. Do you know what gets you into flow? What the trigger is that helps you get into a state of happiness and joy, where your work flows from you like music from a concert violinist? No? Well, buckle up. Pay attention. And get flowing….

INTRODUCTION

When it comes to work and life, are you spending your time doing or being? Of course, we all have to do things. But how are you being when you are doing?

Do you power through your day, doing the best with what you have, only to find yourself physically drained, emotionally empty, and out of flow? Or are you fully in flow, deeply engaged, exceeding your potential—feeling whole, happy, and fulfilled?

As a violinist, playing a high-precision instrument under high pressure, I've learned that when I'm deeply engaged with the music, all the "doingness" seems to disappear and my "beingness" takes me on an amazing ride of self-actualization.

Getting into the music is a musician's version of getting into the flow state, and while the lessons of getting into flow didn't come easily, in the end, not only have I gained flow, I've gained flow mastery.

Now, as a global authority on flow, I empower people in all aspects of their lives to get into their flow on purpose, and with purpose.

Performing faster-higher-louder is a sarcastic comment musicians make about the flashy players who perform without any emotional connection to the music. It's like being a robot instead of being in your humanity. In the workplace, it could be described as lack of engagement, purpose, or even civility.

Nowadays, faster-higher-louder literally describes the current environment. Technology is taking off at lightning speed with people scrambling to expand their skills during the AI revolution. Meanwhile, the pile of global issues continues to stack up higher and higher, and people are getting pretty loud about their stress and frustrations.

It's commonly known that stress narrows cognitive focus and ideation. It can also drain overall energy, and it negatively impacts mental health.

What's not commonly known is that when in flow, focus broadens, thoughts expand, and learning speed increases. Work becomes rewarding to the point where it refuels you, and because you're in flow, it positively impacts mental health.

Getting into your flow state is the entry point to being in a world of doing. It's a way to not only ground yourself in today's environment, but it's a way to tap into your best self, live life with meaning, and go beyond what you've ever imagined.

Flow education is like one-stop shopping to resolve many of today's issues—reconnecting people with the humanity that already exists within them so they can be engaged, unlock their genius, and love what they do.

Whether you are leading yourself, or leading others, you just have to tap into your flow.

I can show you how. Are you ready?

Chapter 1

WHAT'S POSSIBLE?

"Diane Allen… NEXT!" I leave the noisy warm-up room and step into the hallway. It's so quiet, all I can hear is the buzz in my ears and my heartbeat. I walk down the hallway to the audition room. The door opens and the violinist auditioning before me bursts out, avoids all eye contact, and leaves as fast as possible.

I step into the large white room with bright fluorescent lighting and a solitary music stand placed right in the middle. Seated against the wall is a line of judges. I walk up, place my music on the stand, and tune my violin.

"What's your name and what will you be performing for us today?"

It's customary to begin an orchestra audition with a solo piece followed by specific excerpts from the symphonic repertoire. "My name is Diane Allen. I'll be performing the Barber Violin Concerto."

I lift my violin to my shoulder and bring the bow to the strings. What comes out of my violin is beyond anything I have ever experienced in the practice room or at an audition. Instead of the usual shaky fingers and racing heart, my vibrato sounds gorgeous. The bow tone, exquisite. My inner dialog is silent, and my mind has a dreamy quality to it. I'm focused to the point where nothing else exists. My arms and fingers are so nimble they're in complete communion with executing my soul's interpretation of the music. It's euphoric.

As I'm playing an ascending musical pattern, from out of nowhere, my snarky inner critic breaks through my deep focus and says, *How are you going to keep that up?* The pattern was supposed to repeat three times, but my fingers kept repeating the pattern up to the top of the violin. It was awful.

As for what happened next, I can't tell you. That's when the amnesia set in. What I do know is I walked out of the audition early. What I don't know is whether leaving was my decision or the judges'.

How is it possible to go beyond what I thought I was capable of, then grossly underperform, followed by an immediate case of amnesia?

What the heck was that?

I guess that while one part of me was soaring, another part of me was freaking out, resulting in me being the one bursting out of the audition, avoiding all eye contact. It was like plummeting to earth after high-altitude flying with no previous navigation experience.

But how did I come to soar in the first place? I witnessed myself exceeding my potential. I hadn't known this level of performance was even a possibility for me. If that's possible, then what else is possible?

After experiencing the wildest emotional rollercoaster ride ever, I find myself at the intersection of a number of crossroads.

- Do I curl up in a fetal position and hide to protect myself from any more public humiliation?
- Do I toughen up, gain more audition experience, and figure it out on the fly?
- Do I study up on how to quiet my inner critic, and avoid having stage fright?
- Do I give up on my dream of an orchestra job after decades of rigorous violin training?
- Do I change my career and play freelance violin gigs on the side?
- Do I put the violin down altogether?

If you imagine a roundabout at the center of all these crossroads, I found myself driving around and around, experiencing endless thought circles.

Amid the chaos, I did have one stabilizing factor. I had a violin teaching job that I really enjoyed. The best part? It was pressure-free.

Over the next three decades, I ended up circling that roundabout and journeying down each and every one of those crossroads. Along the way, I kept replaying that memory of what it felt like the day I went beyond what I thought was possible.

At first, laying low to recover from my public embarrassment, my analytical mind desperately wanted to gain control over my hyperactive stress response. I learned general things like the importance of staying hydrated for electrical conductivity in the brain, and how regular exercise reduces buildup of the stress hormone cortisol.

Then I learned specifics.

When the fight, flight, or freeze response is triggered, the blood leaves the more developed parts of our brain and floods the amygdala. This is why we forget things in the heat of the moment. As soon as the stress is relieved, the blood is released back into the outer parts of the brain. It's like the light switch gets turned back on and we remember everything we have just forgotten.[1]

But that still doesn't prevent nervous reactions like quivering, nausea, or clammy hands from making their entrance. Turns out that when we're anxious, the Achilles tendon tenses up, getting ready to fight, flee, or freeze. Regularly massaging the Achilles tendon allows it to stay relaxed, communicating to the amygdala, "Hey there! We're all calm down here. Nothing to worry about."

Physical Actions That Prevent Physical Reactions
- Hydration
- Cardio
- Achilles tendon massage

---

[1] Dennison and Dennison, *Brain Gym® Teacher's Edition* (USA: Edu-Kinesthetics Inc., 2010).

When you perform on a high-precision instrument like the violin, and you're doing it under pressure, even the tiniest finger quiver can botch things up. So, I go all out with hydration, exercise, cardio, and daily Achilles tendon massage. This routine makes an enormous difference.

No more amnesia. No more underperforming. I figure it out. This is a big win for my analytical mind and its desire to be in control.

But the vivid memory of that exquisite, magical moment still calls to me. My body had been in complete service to my soul; my abilities and musical interpretation, transcendent. What would it take to experience that again?

> *"If you can dream it, you can be it.
> But if you can experience it,
> you can repeat it."*

The quest was on.

Orchestra concerts become my testing grounds. There's a feeling of safety when you're surrounded by a sea of violinists. The concert environment is the perfect lab in which to experiment with taming my nerves and find my way to awaken the magical moments.

The more control I gain over my stress response, the more I experience flow. At first, it is fleeting. Then more sustained. I find myself relying less and less on my stress-control routine and focusing more on getting into the music.

Getting into the music is a musician's version of getting into the flow state.

According to famed psychologist Mihaly Csikszentmihalyi (pronounced *mee-HIGH CHEEK-sent-me-HIGH-ee)*, flow is a state of complete immersion and focus in an activity, where one loses a sense of time and self-consciousness, experiencing a sense of ease and engagement.

> "The best moments in our lives are not the passive, receptive, relaxing times... The best moments usually occur when a person's body or mind is stretched to its limits in a voluntary effort to accomplish something difficult and worthwhile." [2]

---

[2] Mihaly Csikszentmihalyi, *Flow: The Psychology of Optimal Experience*, (New York: Harper Perennial Modern Classics, 2008).

While my stress-control routine is a stepping-stone, flow is responsible for the magic. Flow makes it possible for me to be deeply engaged, fulfill my heart, and go beyond what I think I am capable of.

I like to describe flow as:

*"When your genius
and your heart become one."*

> Excellence occurs at the intersection of performance and precision. Add passion, and the experience of excellence becomes transcendent, the outcome deeply fulfilling. It's the stuff that self-actualization is made from, and flow is the gateway.

As a violinist, I face achieving excellence daily. As a pilot, my son, Scott, faces achieving excellence daily. As a crane operator, my brother-in-law, Mike, picks up and turns train engines so that mechanics can do their work. Excellence is a must because one ounce of error and that engine starts swinging, quickly becoming fatal.

Of course, not everyone has a no-room-for-error daily challenge that requires them to always be at their peak at a specific moment in time.

That said, people slip in and out of flow naturally without even realizing it.

Have you ever been so focused that you lost complete track of time and felt at one with the activity? Maybe you're cooking, playing pickleball, or lost in an Excel spreadsheet. How about a brainstorming meeting? Did you have ideas and insights come in from out of the blue? Don't you just love it when things fall into place and come together with ease? During these kinds of experiences, you are in flow.

It's like a superpower, and *you* have your own version of it. The problem is most people don't find themselves in flow very often. When you do get there, you're in the middle of a challenge, giving it your undivided attention, and you're rocking your genius. At some point, you look up and wonder, "Huh. Where's the time gone?" Now you're out of flow and you don't know how to get back into that blissful state.

And doesn't it seem like flow is the hardest to get into when you need it the most? Like when you're burned out, out of your comfort zone, or facing constant interruptions?

We may think the flow state is esoteric, that it's for the elite. NOPE. Not true. I've learned over the years that you, too, have experienced that high-altitude flying of flow despite a lack of navigation experience.

But you may have denied that you were in flow. How many times have you said, "It was a lucky moment" or, "Never mind, it was just a pipe dream." Maybe you've anticipated a time when you wanted to be in flow and found yourself saying, "I'm afraid if I prepare, I'll jinx it."

"How are you going to keep that up?" was the question that caused me to crash during that fateful audition.

As I circled the roundabout exploring all the different crossroads, I learned many lessons and made a number of discoveries. But in reality, I was searching for the how-to manual on making flow a repeatable experience.

- What would it be like if you could get into flow on demand?
- Could you soar and exceed your potential?
- What if possibilities you never even knew were possible became real in your life?
- Would you be surprised if I told you that flow is the key to experiencing more meaning, joy, and fulfillment in work and life?
- What would it be like if you could find your flow, unlock your genius, and love what you do?

Your guide for mastering flow is just one page away.

TAKEAWAYS

Flow Defined
Flow is an optimal state of mind when you feel your best and perform your best. It's when your genius and heart become one.

Stress Management Techniques
Hydration, exercise, and Achilles tendon massage help with improving performance under high stress.

Transcendence
Silencing your inner critic (a byproduct of flow) plays a part in experiencing transcendence.

Accessibility of Flow
Flow is not just for elite performers. It's accessible to everyone.

Benefits of Flow
Making flow a repeatable experience helps to both maximize your potential and go beyond what you thought possible.

Path to Fulfillment
Achieving flow leads to greater meaning, joy, and fulfillment in both work and life.

QUESTIONS FOR REFLECTION

Recall Your Flow

- Can you remember a time when you experienced flow?
- What were you doing, and how did it feel?

Stress Management Tools

- What are your current stress management strategies?
- How might hydration, exercise, or Achilles tendon massage improve your routine?

Inner Critic Influence

- How does your inner critic affect you during high-pressure situations?
- What steps can you take to quiet this voice and maintain focus?

Exceeding Expectations

- Think of a moment when you surpassed your own expectations.
- What factors contributed to this, and how can you recreate those conditions?

Applying Flow Professionally

❑ How can you integrate the concept of flow into your professional life?
❑ What changes could help you achieve this state more often?

Career Crossroads

❑ Reflect on any major decisions you're currently facing in your career or personal life.
❑ How might achieving flow influence your choices?

Chapter 2
WHAT IS FLOW?

The flow state falls under the umbrella of positive psychology. Martin Seligman, the father of positive psychology, introduced the concept as a reaction to traditional psychology's focus on negative thinking and mental illness. Coining the term *flow state,* Seligman's concept of "the good life" is one where you use your signature strengths daily as a means of accessing authentic happiness and an abundance of gratification.[3]

> In my experience, to discover your unique way of entering a state of flow, is to discover your unique signature strength. This is your superpower. It's what makes you tick.

---

[3] *Positive Psychology* Wikipedia https://en.wikipedia.org/wiki/Positive_psychology

While Seligman coined the term *flow,* Mihaly Csikszentmihalyi was the first psychologist to conduct in-depth research on flow.

A loose description of how Csikszentmihalyi describes flow is: An optimal state of mind when you feel your best and perform your best.

> My personal interpretation—when your genius and heart become one—lies at the intersection of intellect and passion.

People in flow are deeply focused, fully engaged, highly productive, creative, experiencing peak performance, flourishing, and happy. In addition, we experience all of this in a way that refuels rather than drains us.

Csikszentmihalyi discovered that flow is not just for athletes and people in the arts. His research verified that most people getting into their flow state are actually going through the business of their day-to-day lives.

If that's the case, why aren't more people getting into flow? Especially at the workplace. What's the missing piece?

While there are many components involved, a little education goes a long way. It's my intention to close the gaps and provide you with everything you need so you can develop a healthy relationship with your flow state and make the most of it.

Key Components for Integrating Flow

Flow Education: Learn the neuroscience of flow and how it supports you to thrive.

Flow Awareness: Increase your ability to recognize when you're in flow.

Flow Value: Hold the benefits of flow in high regard.

Flow Activation: Utilize practical strategies to enter into a state of flow.

Flow Culture™: Foster environments conducive to flow states.

Flow Prioritization: Identify flow as vitally important for success and fulfillment in work and life.

For starters, flow is not about learning a different way to think. It's about learning to think differently about being in your natural state of flow. Flow isn't a mindset. It's a mind state. Here's why.

Neuroscientists have discovered that a release of peak-performance hormones creates brain waves conducive to the flow state. The neocortex amps up, dramatically increasing learning speed. The prefrontal cortex temporarily shuts down. This is why we lose a sense of time and a sense of self, key indicators that we are in the flow state. These neurobiological conditions make things like creativity and outstanding performance readily available.

REALIZE

Developing your ability to realize when you are in flow is the first step in being able to get into flow, on demand. People slip in and out of flow naturally. Knowing the six key indicators of flow will help you to realize when you're in it,

1. Lose a Sense of Time

Have you ever noticed that you lose all sense of time when you love what you're doing?

2. Lose a Sense of Self

What does that even mean? When we're in flow, some things get turned on in our brains and others get turned off.

The hormones that get turned on are endorphins, dopamine, serotonin, norepinephrine, anandamide. Because of this, we experience euphoria, motivation, peak performance, and happiness.[4]

Here's what gets turned off: your inner critic and your fight, flight, or freeze response. As a result, fear and negative self-talk won't get in your way. That's why people find flow so liberating and say things like, "I find myself by losing myself in the activity," and my favorite, "I'm not doing. I'm being."

---

4   Steven Kotler *How to Hack Your Brain* (for $5000) New York Times (2017) https://www.nytimes.com/2017/09/21/style/what-is-flow.htmll

The Impact of Hormones on Flow State

Endorphins: Euphoria and Determination

Dopamine: Motivation and Performance

Serotonin: Happiness

Norepinephrine: Peak Performance and Rise to the Occasion

3. Ideas and Insights Come from Out of the Blue

A whopping 95 percent of our thoughts are repeating. When you're in flow, you have new thoughts.

4. Things Come Together with a Sense of Ease

You know those times when you get way more done in 30 minutes than you had in the last three days? That's flow in action.

5. Experience a Positive Feedback Loop

When you pour yourself into your work, a task, or a project, and there's no energy coming back, your work drains you and you get into a negative feedback loop. When you work in flow, your effort is so rewarding that it refuels you and you get into a positive feedback loop.

The Impact of Flow on Personal Fulfillment

6. Experience More Meaning, Joy, and Fulfillment

Imagine feeling your best, performing at your best, and even going beyond what you ever thought possible. That's what flourishing is all about.

On the mental health spectrum, halfway between depression and flourishing, there's this midway point where you're fine but you're not fine. You're *functional* but you can't get motivated. You're just blah. The word for that? Languishing. Languishing in mental health is when you feel stuck and empty. While you may not have a diagnosable mental illness, you recognize that you've been feeling off for a sustained period of time. [5,6]

According to organizational psychologist Adam Grant, languishing was the predominant emotion one year into the pandemic. How do you go from languishing to flourishing? Grant specifically states that the antidote is flow. [7,8]

---

5 Keyes, C. L. M., "The Mental Health Continuum: From Languishing to Flourishing in Life." *Journal of Health and Social Behavior*, no. 43(2) (June, 2002): 207-222.

6 Seligman, M. E. P., *Flourish: A Visionary New Understanding of Happiness and Well-being.* (New York: Free Press, 2011).

7 Adam Grant, "Feeling Blah During the Pandemic? It's Called Languishing." *New York Times* (April 19, 2021), https://www.nytimes.com/2021/04/19/well/mind/covid-mental-health-languishing.html.

8 Adam Grant, "How to Stop Languishing and Start Finding Flow," filmed August, 2021 at TEDMonterey), https://www.ted.com/talks/adam_grant_how_to_stop_languishing_and_start_finding_flow.

Beyond Engagement™: Flow for Mental Health and Happiness

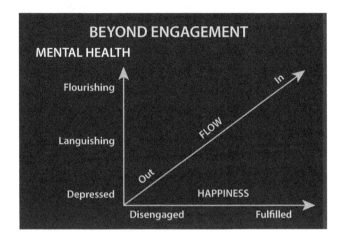

So, what just happened as you read through these key indicators of flow? Were you remembering times when you've been in flow? Were you reflecting on your own experiences of being in a negative or positive feedback loop? Did you gain perspective on past performance successes or failures? Did you find yourself longing for more focus, productivity, creativity, meaning, joy, or fulfillment?

If so, say hello to flow awareness. This is just the type of self-reflection necessary for you to develop your ability to access flow more frequently.

If you found yourself longing for outcomes like deep focus or increased creativity, then you discovered the flow values that are most important to you.

In reference to neuroscience supporting you to thrive, do you see how a statement like "go with the flow" is a mindset, and how "being in your flow state" is a mind state? In other words, the flow state is a real thing. Not only is it real, but it can also be cultivated.

Recently, my husband and I went out to enjoy some music. The place was packed. It was a typical rock band with two guitars, bass, drums, and a lead singer, and would you look at that! The lead singer and guitarist is a former student of mine. Shaene. As a student, Shaene was timid, quiet, and performed with no emotion. Now, she's rocking the stage, and singing her heart out. When I spoke with her afterward, she said, "I still use everything I learned from you. It just took me a while to grow into it."

As you deepen your flow awareness, you may find an immediate connection to it, or like Shaene, it may take some time for you to grow into it.

But it all starts with you remembering a time when you were in flow.

- Maybe you can remember a time when you were completely in flow.
- Maybe you can remember a time when you were kind of in flow.
- Or anywhere in between. Simply note which specific memory comes up for you.

With that memory in mind, you are now ready for flow activation.

TAKEAWAYS

Positive Psychology
Flow aims to optimize your signature strengths as a means of achieving happiness and gratification.

Flow Characteristics
- Focused
- Engaged
- Productive
- Creative
- In Peak Performance
- Flourishing
- Happy

Neuroscience of Flow: Hormones and Their Impact on Flow State
- **Endorphins:** Euphoria and determination
- **Dopamine:** Motivation and performance
- **Serotonin:** Happiness
- **Norepinephrine:** Peak performance, rise to the occasion
- **Anandamide:** Bliss

Flow Awareness: Key Indicators of Flow
- **Losing a Sense of Time:** Immersion and joy
- **Losing a Sense of Self:** Silenced inner critic and fearlessness
- **Ideas and Insights:** Generate new thoughts
- **Ease:** Things fall easily into place
- **Positive Feedback Loop:** Refuels
- **Joy and Fulfillment:** Thrive and flourish

Flow Values

The characteristics of flow that you value the most.

QUESTIONS FOR REFLECTION

Personal Flow Moments

- ❏ Reflect on a specific time when you experienced flow.
- ❏ What were you doing, and how did it feel?

Indicators of Flow

- ❏ Which key indicators of flow have you experienced? (Losing a sense of time, losing a sense of self, new ideas and insights, ease, positive feedback loop, meaning, joy, happiness.)
- ❏ How did they manifest in your activities?

Flow in Daily Activities

- ❏ How can you incorporate the concept of flow into your everyday tasks professionally and personally?

Neuroscience Insights

- ❏ How does understanding the neuroscience behind flow help you to recognize and achieve this state?

Transforming States

- Have you experienced languishing?
- How might achieving flow help you move toward flourishing?

Flow Values

- What aspects of flow (e.g., deep focus, creativity, productivity, peak performance, happiness) are most important to you?
- How can you cultivate these in your life?

Chapter 3

DISCOVER YOUR FLOW STRATEGY™

As a violinist, losing myself by getting into the music has been my answer for everything. I had no idea why, but that's how I overcame obstacles like shyness and audition anxiety.

That's how I found fulfillment in my work.

That's how I learned how to lead.

Without the flow state, I never would have been able to play my best as the concertmaster of the Central Oregon Symphony.

My performance anxiety started the day of my Philadelphia Youth Orchestra audition.

The warm-up room is packed with people practicing everywhere. I open my violin case, pull out my violin, and it slips out of my hands, lands face down on the hard tile floor, and pieces fly in all directions.

The entire room goes silent.

I turn the violin back over and discover that it actually didn't break. So, I get busy reassembling it. I put the pegs back in, restring the violin, and place the bridge back under the strings. Just as I get it tuned, they call my name to go and audition. No warming up for me! Not only does my violin sound horrible from the fall, but my hands are shaky and cold. I couldn't be any further away from flow. So embarrassing! Somehow, I am still accepted to be a member of the orchestra, but due to my poor performance, I've been relegated to the last chair of the violin section.

During my college years, I still can't shake off my performance nerves. Each year in school, I must take a "jury." A jury is an evaluative performance where a student performs before a panel of faculty members. The panel assesses the student's technical and artistic development and provides feedback. It's like a final exam. Each time, my nerves get the better part of me. Similar to how I still got into the youth orchestra—sitting last chair—the college violin faculty gives me poor marks but still awards me a bachelor's and master's degree in violin performance. Bottom line, there's a huge performance gap between being a well-trained violinist and displaying my abilities under pressure.

I'm now 34 years old, an exhausted mom to my newborn son, Scott, and I haven't practiced in weeks. For the third year in a row, I see an ad for a teaching job in Central Oregon. For whatever reason, I decide to go for it.

So, I'm at the audition, and from out of the blue, as luck would have it, I find myself going to that place where all my hard work, practice, and passion magically come to life. I'm so immersed in the music that underneath my fingers the violin seems to sing by itself. During this three-hour teaching demonstration, the students respond well to my spontaneous creative solutions. In the audience are students, parents, teachers, musicians, and, to my surprise, the conductor of the local symphony orchestra. The daylong marathon feels like it goes by in five minutes. Not only do they offer me the job on the spot, but shortly after we relocate from Cleveland, Ohio to our new home in Bend, Oregon, I'm asked to sit first chair of the Central Oregon Symphony.

All my dormant skills come alive, and it's incredibly rewarding to finally be able to put all my training and passion to full use.

The concertmaster is the lead violinist and second in command to the conductor. Imagine if I was just sitting there being nervous and going through the motions. Think of what a huge disservice that would be for both the orchestra and the audience. I didn't have a choice. I had to get into the music.

So how does a musician get into the music and into their flow state? Most of us have a hard time describing it. You'd think we were talking about a magic trick.

"I feel it."

"It's like I'm singing."

"It just happens to me."

Flow has a reputation for being tricky. Tricky to get into and tricky to maintain. For me personally, as I got into flow more often, I started to notice things. The more I get into the music, the better I play, and the better I play, the more I get into the music. It's a positive feedback loop, within myself.

Then I noticed the same positive feedback loop occurs when I'm teaching my violin students, just in a different way. The more I get into the music, the more my students get into the music. Flow made leading by example irresistible, effective, and fun.

Imagine, little kiddos, rocking it, at the recital. The students are inspiring each other to do personal bests. The parents, dabbing tears from their eyes, attend standing-room-only violin recitals year after year after year.

I never had to do sales to recruit new students. I always had a waiting list. This was my workplace culture.

While I didn't know it at the time, I was actually teaching my students how to get into flow.

In my role as the concertmaster, leading with flow sparked a synergistic state of group flow for both the orchestra and the audience.

With hundreds of rock-solid performances under my belt, turning on that light switch and tapping into flow became routine. Except for this one concert, when I spontaneously decide to marry my two loves of public speaking and playing the violin.

I'm having a really good time giving the pre-concert lecture. I turn around, sit down, and give a big cue for the music to start. Only, I can't move. My elbows are frozen. While it feels like an hour, it only takes about a minute for me to regain the full use of my arms. But now there's a disconnect. I'm not putting any feeling into the music. It's like I've forgotten how.

That can't ever happen again!

My first thought is that I'm having a transition issue, going from speaking to the audience to playing the violin. But it's actually about the shift from being out of flow into the flow state. I must find a way to shift into flow and to be able to do it on purpose. My reputation and job security depend on it.

That night, after the concert, I'm sitting on the couch feeling humiliated and grilling myself with questions. I do get into my flow state in a variety of places. On stage is **WHERE** it happens the most. But **WHAT** am I doing? Of course, I'm playing the violin. That's what I'm doing on the outside. **WHAT** am I doing on the inside? My friends would say, "Diane, we're creating the music." And I get that. To me, however, it feels more like sharing. I'm sharing the message of the music, and I'm sharing the experience.

Well, that feels right!

But what about those concerts when I'm moved to tears? It's like the flow state on steroids. I always cry during audience singalongs. The orchestra members have to squish together so the choir can fit on stage behind us. A packed house with the house lights turned all the way up lies in front of the orchestra. Between the audience and the choir singing their hearts out, along with the orchestra in all its glory, there's so much sound you can feel your bones vibrating to the music. And there I am, sitting on stage with my head turned sideways to keep the steady stream of tears from falling onto my antique violin and damaging the finish. Something about a large group of people coming together through the music taps me into this uncontrollable emotional reaction. **WHY?** Why is it so meaningful? Unity. Unifying large groups of people through one activity always touches me to the core. I experience that same response when I participate with thousands of people at the Walk to End Alzheimer's fundraiser.

Back to the concert when my elbows froze. All I could think was, "Just keep moving, just keep moving, just keep moving." I bet if I had known to focus on sharing and creating unity, I could have gotten into the music.

Well, there's nothing like the sting of embarrassment to give you a kick in the pants. Because of all this personal self-reflection, the performance-fail ended up being a good thing. It allowed me to discover my Flow Strategy™.

Sharing is how I shift into the flow state *on purpose.* Unity is how I can shift into it *with purpose.*

FLOW STRATEGY™

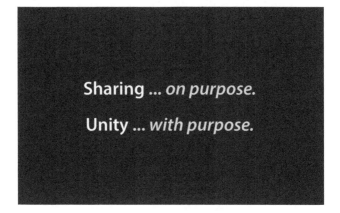

Sharing ... *on purpose.*

Unity ... *with purpose.*

So, the question is, "Do you just have to sit around and wait for it to happen?"

Not when you can discover your own Flow Strategy™ and tap into your heartfelt genius.

Discover Your Flow Strategy™
Now it's your turn to discover your Flow Strategy™

Previously, we talked about flow awareness. The main point of awareness is to realize when you're actually in flow. That's a prerequisite for flow activation.

Because people slip in and out of flow naturally, remembering the key indicators will help you to realize when you're in it.

To review, the key indicators of being in flow are:

- Losing a sense of time.
- Losing a sense of self.
- Ideas and insights coming from out of the blue.
- Things coming together with a sense of ease.
- Being in a positive feedback loop.
- Experiencing more meaning, joy, and fulfillment.

Recreating a memory of being in flow is the first step in discovering your own unique way of entering a state of flow.

With a memory in mind, the next step toward flow activation is to analyze your own unique Flow Strategy™.

That night, when I was trying to figure out if I could get into flow on demand, it took three questions to unlock my flow. The same three questions will help you find your flow, unlock genius, and love what you do.

1. Ask yourself: "WHERE? Where am I when I get into the flow state the most?"

Notice everything about the location and the environmental factors that are conducive for you to get into flow. Is it quiet or bustling? Does it smell of coffee? Are you listening to your favorite music?

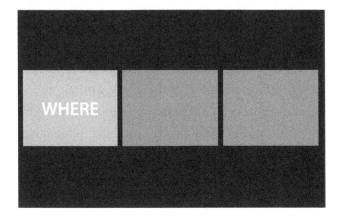

2. Now ask "WHAT? What am I doing on the outside and on the inside?"

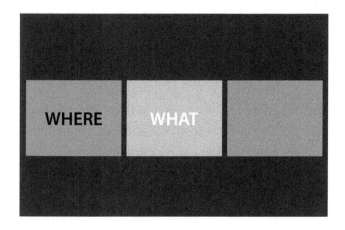

If "WHERE" you get into the flow state the most at home is in the kitchen, "WHAT" you're doing on the outside is the activity: cooking, baking, washing dishes, etc. "WHAT" you're doing on the inside is what you personally bring to the activity. This is unique to you. On the inside, you could be experimenting, meditating, or nurturing the people you're cooking for.

If "WHERE" you get into the flow state the most is in your office, on the outside, you're working on an Excel spreadsheet. On the inside, you could be doing any number of things: problem-solving, visualizing, strategizing, etc.

3. Now ask "WHY? Why is it so meaningful?"

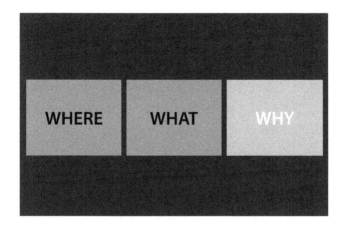

Going back to our previous example:

- WHERE you mostly get into the flow state is in the kitchen.
- WHAT you're doing on the outside is cooking. WHAT you're doing on the inside is nurturing.
- Now ask "WHY? Why is what you're doing on the inside so meaningful?" Ask WHY over and over again until you reach the high ideals you value the most. These are intrinsic values like peace, love, joy, well-being, equality, freedom, etc.

For example:

- "WHY is it so meaningful for me to be nurturing?"
  - "Because I want the best for my kids."
- "WHY do I want the best for my kids?"
  - "Because I want them to be healthy and strong."
- "WHY do I want them to be healthy and strong?"
  - "Because I love them so much."

What you do on the inside is your most compelling internal self-motivator. Knowing what you do on the inside means you can now shift into the flow state *on purpose.*

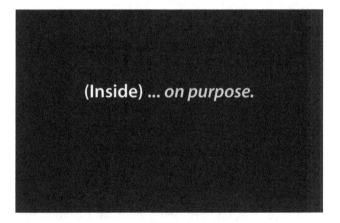

Why the activity is so meaningful is your most compelling external self-motivator. Knowing why it's so meaningful means you can now shift into the flow state *with purpose.*

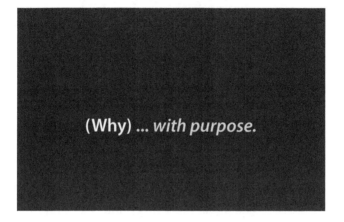

(Why) ... *with purpose.*

Flow Strategy™

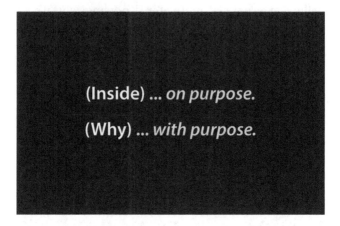

This is your Flow Strategy™:

- WHAT you do on the inside is how you shift into the flow state *on purpose*.
- WHY it's so meaningful is how you shift into the flow state *with purpose*.

Cooking Example:
- Nurturing is how I shift into the flow state *on purpose*.
- Love and well-being are how I shift into the flow state *with purpose*.

This is your unique way of connecting what you love with what you do.

My Flow Strategy™ Worksheet

WHERE I get into my flow state the most:

....
....
....

WHAT I'm doing on the outside:

....
....
....

WHAT I'm doing on the inside:

....
....
....

WHY it is so meaningful:

....
....
....

My Flow Strategy™

(What I do on the inside)
....

is how I shift into the flow state *on purpose.*

(Why it is so meaningful)
....

is how I can shift into the flow state *with purpose.*

diane@dianeallen.com | DianeAllen.com | All Rights Reserved

Figuring out my Flow Strategy™ was one thing. Utilizing it was another. As a violinist, I never had to network. But as I explored a career in public speaking, networking was something I had to do even though I didn't care for it. It was so awkward. People standing around in tight circles. Me, trying to break into the conversations. It was like middle school all over again. One time I got so frustrated, I locked myself in the bathroom stall to regroup. Then it came to me. I went back out and listened to the context of each conversation. If I had something relevant to say, I'd share it along with a story. The stories sparked fun conversations and opened people up to share their stories. Sharing is how I shift into the flow state on purpose. Suddenly, I felt like myself again. I couldn't believe it, but I actually ran out of business cards.

I went beyond what I thought possible. I had no idea my Flow Strategy™ for performing music would work somewhere else and help me to get outside my comfort zone. The outcome of sharing the stories was that I was able to connect. Since connection is unifying, I was able to get into it with purpose.

Now you know the next step to flow activation: Utilize your Flow Strategy™.

I was giving a workshop on peak performance. One of the managers in attendance had flat-out refused to publicly present a status report at the annual company-wide meeting. His job fills the entire pipeline of the company. He's the land acquisition manager for a real estate developer and his absence on the annual meeting stage does not give people confidence for what's coming down the pipeline. Clearly, his aversion to public speaking would not serve him well. We needed to figure out how he could tap into a flow state rather than allowing his nerves to get the better of him.

More conversation revealed that he gets into his flow state the most when bicycle racing. On the outside, he's dressed in spandex, riding his super cool bike. On the inside, he's selflessly supporting the team as if their lives depend on it. The team collaboration lights his fire and explains why he finds bike racing so meaningful.

Figuring out his Flow Strategy™ changed everything. Now, he had a good reason to stand in front of 250 people and review the status report. He wanted to support his co-workers and create team synergy.

Not only do we each have our own unique Flow Strategies™, but we also have our own unique way of using them. After I'd given a talk to a room full of scientists, one of them beelined to me and asked, "How is this going to help me in the boardroom?" I asked her the Flow Strategy™ questions I outlined in this chapter. It turns out that she gets into the flow state most in the lab. On the outside, she's using her hands. On the inside, she's discovering. Why it's so meaningful is because she's contributing to the expansion of knowledge.

Then I asked, "Is there some way you can use your hands in the boardroom?"

Aha!

She has since earned a reputation for livening up the meetings. She brings in props and models and purposefully uses her hands. By using what she does on the outside, she taps right into what she does on the inside: discovering. Being in her spirit of discovering is an amazing asset to have in the boardroom.

Flow Awareness + Flow Activation

REALIZE when you're in flow.

ANALYZE your flow state memories to figure out your unique Flow Strategy™.

UTILIZE your Flow Strategy™ to get into flow, on demand.

Can you have more than one Flow Strategy™? Absolutely! When I'm composing music, WHERE I am is in my home office. WHAT I'm doing on the outside: composing. WHAT I'm doing on the inside: problem-solving. WHY it's so meaningful: freedom of expression. Problem-solving is how I get into my flow state *on purpose*. Freedom of expression is how I can shift into my flow state *with purpose*.

For some people, the environment (WHERE they are) plays a big part when it comes to their ability to get into flow. A gentleman who heard me speak at a human resources conference scheduled a call. When we got on the phone, he told me he was very motivated to increase the amount of time he spent in flow at the workplace. Only, he couldn't remember a single time when he had been in flow.

I told him I'd peeked at his LinkedIn profile right before the call and saw his claim to fame: *avid skier – mediocre golfer.* "Well, of course I get into flow when I ski. Just not at work."

Clearly, his WHERE is on the ski slopes. I asked if there was anything in particular about the environment. "First, I do a thorough cleaning of my goggles. Then, I set up my playlist, pop in my earbuds, and start the music just in time to jump off the lift. On the way down, I become one with the snow, lose all sense of time, and feel free."

Without skipping a beat, he realized that whenever he does his best work, it's because, like skiing, he's set up a time block for a specific task. Instead of cleaning his goggles, he organizes his desk, and in both cases, he queues up a playlist.

That's flow awareness in action. This has given him the ability to tap into flow at work.

Time of day, another aspect of environment, can also impede or invite flow. I was coaching a video editor during the pandemic lockdown, a chaotic time when both he and his wife were working from home and caring for their toddler. Similar to the day I couldn't get into the music, he lost his artistry. To minimize the working-from-home chaos, the couple was following a strict schedule. Only, the schedule didn't take into account that the video editor is a night owl. The husband was visibly relieved on the Zoom call when we agreed it was time to shake up that strict schedule and go with the flow so he could be in flow. Remember, *go with the flow is a mindset; being in your flow* is a mind state.

Using your Flow Strategy™ goes far, but it's not the only technique for flow activation.

There's also a universal entry point into flow that brings out the best in all of us.

TAKEAWAYS

Flow Awareness

Use the key indicators of being in flow as the first step in figuring out your Flow Strategy™.

Discover Your Flow Strategy™

Reverse engineer how you uniquely get into flow by using the three-step Flow Strategy™ system.

Three-Step Flow Strategy™ System

- **WHERE?** Where are you when you get into the flow state the most?
- **WHAT?** What are you doing on the outside, and on the inside?
- **WHY?** Why is the activity so meaningful?

This is your Flow Strategy™

- What you do on the inside is how you shift into flow *on purpose.*
- Why it's so meaningful is how you can shift into flow *with purpose.*

Flow Activation

Utilize your Flow Strategy™ to get into your flow state.

QUESTIONS FOR REFLECTION

Experiencing Performance Gaps

- Reflect on a time when you underperformed and notice the decisions you made as a result of misrepresenting what you were capable of.
- Are there any dormant skills you'd like to reawaken?
- What would change for you if you closed current gaps and went beyond what you thought possible?

Flow Strategy™

- Were you able to figure out your Flow Strategy™? Do you need more time to think about it, or time to grow into it?
- **WHERE:** Does a specific environment make a difference for you?
- **WHAT:** Can you see how knowing what you do on the inside benefits you?
- **WHY:** How can you increase a sense of purpose in your daily activities?

Flow Activation

- With your Flow Strategy™ defined, what insights do you have?
- How do you see yourself using that information going forward?

Chapter 4

IGNITE FLOW

Let's get you into flow right now.

I'm going to outline an activity for you to do. That means you won't be imagining the activity. You actually have to do it to learn from it.

As you do the activity, some parts will be easy, other parts will seem impossible, and everything else will be somewhere in between. No matter what, you must experience the successes and the failures because that's the only way you'll be able to benefit from the exercise.

> First, read all the directions up to the statement that says *Begin*.
>
> Find a location where you can be alone and uninterrupted.

Do each item on the list of actions below until you are successful. When you reach success, continue the action for a bit longer before you pause and go on to the next prompt.

You may or may not get through this entire list. It doesn't matter. Go until things fall apart and then go back a step or two and give the steps more time to gel. What does matter is that you stay in the game with a curious mind and observe how you're reacting to the situation.

- Pat your head with your hand with an up-and-down motion.
- With your other hand, rub your tummy in circles. (No head patting.)
- Pat your head again. Now add rubbing your tummy.
- Continue patting your head. As you rub your tummy, reverse the direction of the circle.
- Keep going with both hands and increase your speed.
- Keep going. Add mental math spoken out loud: 3 + 5 + 3 + 5 etc. (3 + 5 = 8 + 3 = 11 + 5 = 16, etc.)

- SWITCH HANDS. Pat your head with your other hand in an up-and-down motion.
- With your other hand, rub your tummy in circles. (No head patting.)
- Pat your head again. Now add rubbing your tummy.
- Continue patting your head. As you rub your tummy, reverse the direction of the circle.
- Keep going with both hands and increase your speed.
- Keep going. Add mental math spoken out loud: 3 + 5 + 3 + 5, etc. (3 + 5 = 8 + 3 = 11 + 5 = 16, etc.)

Set a timer for five minutes. Begin and don't stop no matter what. When the timer goes off, stop. Then read the next set of instructions.

Begin.

Now that you get the gist of the activity, let's take it to a new level.

Role-play being a volunteer who entertains children in the cancer ward of a hospital. One of the many ways you entertain them is by patting your head and rubbing your tummy while doing math. The children get to watch your successes and your failures and everything in between.

Repeat the list of actions on the previous page. Start from the top so the children can see you experience the progression. As you go through the actions, visualize the experience.

- What does the room look like?
- What do the children look like?
- What kinds of things do they spontaneously call out while you're doing the activities?
- Are they silent?
- Laughing?
- Think about what you're doing as a metaphor designed to inspire the children to overcome their hardships.

Set your timer for five minutes.

Begin.

How was it?

- Did the time fly by?
- Did the time go by slowly, but in a good way?
- Was your inner critic silent? Noisy? A mixture of both?
- Did you want to stop, and/or did you sense yourself rise to the occasion?
- Did you find the added challenges satisfying in some way?
- Did role-playing a volunteer at a cancer ward take this to a whole other dimension?

Patting your head and rubbing your belly—these are skills.

Patting your head and rubbing your belly at the same time, reversing the circle, going faster, switching hands, and doing mental math—these are challenges.

According to Csikszentmihalyi, at the intersection of skill and challenge is when flow ignites. It's the universal entry point into flow.

Think of a skill without a challenge. Nothing will become ignited.

Think of a challenge without a skill. Nothing will become ignited.

It's at the intersection of the two that ignites the magic of flow.

The Universal Entry Point into Flow

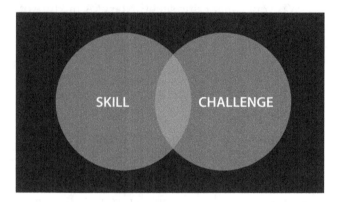

Volunteering to entertain children at a cancer ward was the *purpose*.

As you noticed, *purpose* elevates the experience and takes it to a new dimension.

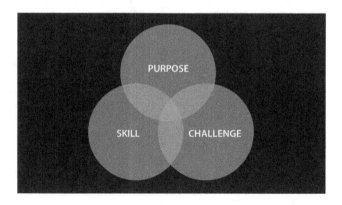

Have you ever noticed how rewarding it is to do volunteer work? There's a group of people with a variety of skills, facing the challenges together, and doing it all for a purpose.

Creating the same rewarding experiences throughout your work and life is the end game.

But first, let's go deeper.

I want you to imagine the circles as dials. These dials indicate the range between under-skilled and over-skilled as well as the range between under-challenged and over-challenged.

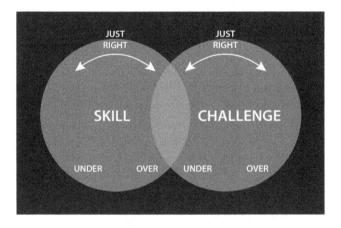

Going back to the skills of patting, rubbing, and mental math, how would you rate your experience?

For example, here's how I'd rate my experience:

Task	Skill	Challenge
Pat your head with your hand with an up-and-down motion.	WAY OVER-SKILLED	WAY UNDER-CHALLENGED
With your other hand, rub your tummy in circles. (No head patting.)	WAY OVER-SKILLED	WAY UNDER-CHALLENGED
Pat your head again. Now add rubbing your tummy.	COMPETENT SKILL	UNDER-CHALLENGED
Continue patting your head. As you rub your tummy, reverse the direction of the circle.	COMPETENT SKILL	SOME CHALLENGE

Instruction	Skill	Challenge
Keep going with both hands and increase your speed.	COMPETENT SKILL	MODERATE CHALLENGE
Keep going. Add mental math spoken out loud: 3 + 5 + 3 + 5 etc.	COMPETENT SKILL	WAY OVER-CHALLENGED
SWITCH HANDS. Pat your head with your other hand in an up-and-down motion.	WAY OVER-SKILLED	WAY UNDER-CHALLENGED
With your other hand, rub your tummy in circles. (No head patting.)	WAY OVER-SKILLED	WAY UNDER-CHALLENGED
Pat your head again. Now add rubbing your tummy.	COMPETENT SKILL	SOME CHALLENGE
Continue patting your head. As you rub your tummy, reverse the direction of the circle.	SOME SKILL	SOME CHALLENGE
Keep going with both hands and increase your speed.	SOME SKILL	MODERATE CHALLENGE
Keep going. Add mental math spoken out loud: 3 + 5 + 3 + 5 etc.	UNDER-SKILLED	WAY OVER-CHALLENGED

Ignite Flow

How would you rate yours?

Pat your head with your hand with an up-and-down motion.	
With your other hand, rub your tummy in circles. (No head patting.)	
Pat your head again. Now add rubbing your tummy.	
Continue patting your head. As you rub your tummy, reverse the direction of the circle.	
Keep going with both hands and increase your speed.	
Keep going. Add mental math spoken out loud: 3 + 5 + 3 + 5, etc.	
SWITCH HANDS. Pat your head with your other hand in an up-and-down motion.	
With your other hand, rub your tummy in circles. (No head patting.)	

Pat your head again. Now add rubbing your tummy.	
Continue patting your head. As you rub your tummy, reverse the direction of the circle.	
Keep going with both hands and increase your speed.	
Keep going. Add mental math spoken out loud: 3 + 5 + 3 + 5, etc.	

Remember the emotions you had when you first went through all the variations of patting your head and rubbing your tummy? Thinking of these circles as dials provides you with an assessment tool. That means you now have the opportunity to zoom out of your emotions and look at your performance objectively.

> To ignite flow, you have to push just beyond your comfort zone. That's the sweet spot that ignites flow, setting the stage to go beyond what you thought was possible.

While this is subjective, here are some examples of the sweet spot:

UNDER-SKILLED   SOME CHALLENGE   COMPETENT SKILL   MODERATE CHALLENGE

Examples of how to adjust to find the sweet spot:

Change   to

WAY OVER-SKILLED   UNDER-CHALLENGED   WAY OVER-SKILLED   MODERATE CHALLENGE

Change   to

UNDER-SKILLED   WAY OVER-CHALLENGED   UNDER-SKILLED   SOME CHALLENGE

Keep in mind that the challenge that brings out the best is different for everyone. One person's big, hairy, audacious goal will make another person crumble. The key here is to find the right levels that draw out the best in you and/or others.

Returning to the idea of flow being ignited at the intersection of skill, challenge, and purpose, you can use this as both an assessment and a planning tool.

Let's start with assessment.

In a workshop with a group of human resources leaders, a woman said, "I knowingly hired someone overqualified for the job, and I've been nervous about retaining her. Now I know I just need to sit down with her and ask if she'd like to learn any new skills, or if there are challenges she really enjoys."

A team of high school math teachers had been tasked with developing curriculum that teenage math students could relate to. In a training session, the educators told me they had lost their creative spark. The teachers were all highly skilled, and the purpose was clear and compelling: empower students to engage in math. But when we looked at the curriculum the teachers had developed to that point, we discovered they weren't clear about what their current challenges were. So, we took the time to define them. Identifying those challenges sparked a highly productive brainstorming session and a synergistic state of group flow.

Now let's look at planning.

In another session with human resources leaders, a woman shared this insight: "Learning a new skill is challenging. Purpose keeps you motivated. But once the skill has been mastered, you have to create a new plan. How can you bring more challenge to the skill and what new purposes can it serve?"

In work and in life, we often have to use the same skill over and over again. And, yes, that can get downright tedious unless we find a way to change that. When I'm faced with conquering my email inbox (something I'm overly skilled at), for example, I procrastinate for days. But if I give myself until 10:30 a.m. to get through it all, the challenge gets me going and before I know it, not only do I finish by 10:27 a.m., but as I'm answering emails, I usually find ways to create meaningful conversations. There's nothing like a sense of purpose to melt away the doldrums of routine work.

> The key is to make sure that your skills are always challenged, your challenges are always skilled, and there's a clearly defined purpose.

TAKEAWAYS

The Universal Entry Point into Flow

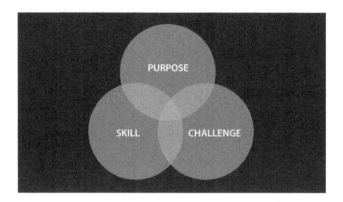

- Flow ignites at the intersection of skill and challenge.
- Purpose elevates the entire experience.
- To ignite flow, you have to push just beyond your comfort zone.

Igniting Flow

Use the universal entry point into flow as both an assessment tool and a planning tool.

QUESTIONS FOR REFLECTION

Activity Experience

- How did you feel while performing the head patting and tummy rubbing activity?
- Did you find it frustrating, satisfying, enjoyable?

Skill and Challenge Balance

- Reflect on the balance between your skills and the challenges you face in your daily life.
- How can adjusting the levels affect your ability to enter flow?

Purpose

- What insights do you have about the role purpose plays for yourself or others?

Applying Flow to Routine Tasks

- How can you apply the concept of the universal entry point into flow toward mundane tasks, making them more engaging and meaningful?

Coaching Others

❑ How can you use the insights from this chapter to help individuals and teams find their flow?

Chapter 5

LEAD WITH FLOW

Growing up as the youngest in my family, including all my first cousins, I remember watching the familial show. I specifically looked to see what the other kids were doing and how they behaved. Then, I'd watch the parents to see their reactions. Based on this, I picked and chose how I wanted to be as a person.

Professional orchestras became another learning environment. All I had to do was watch the show.

After college, the struggle to audition well still plagued me. Not only did I perform freelance in orchestras, but I continued to receive the assignment of sitting last chair of the violin section. That's like being picked last for dodgeball.

On the one hand, this was embarrassing. On the other hand, it gave me the exact same vantage point I had when I was growing up, because I could see all the other violinists. So, I watched the show. Based on what I saw, I would pick and choose the techniques, the body language, and the attitudes I liked the most, along with the behaviors I thought were the most professional. Looking back, I realize that I was actively conceptualizing my leadership style.

With my leadership style already intact, I hit the ground running when I became the concertmaster of the Central Oregon Symphony. As someone who used to sit wide-eyed in the back of the orchestra, one thing I knew for sure was that I, too, would be watched not just by the audience, but by the orchestra members as well.

Having all eyes on me was a challenge I absolutely loved. I wanted to pour my heart and soul into the music and lead both the musicians and the audience to do the same. Because sharing is how I shift into my flow state *on purpose*, and unity is how I can shift into the flow state *with purpose*, I focused deeply on my musical interpretation, and shared it through my violin sound and my physical gestures. Since music is a universal language, I was deeply moved by the way music unites us all.

It was like I was dancing with my Flow Strategy™ and the universal entry point into flow. I even returned to my old routine of drinking lots of water, increasing my blood flow, and rubbing my Achilles.

Think of the energy you've witnessed when an athlete was at the moment of breaking a previous record. Think of the energy you received when you heard a speech, sermon, or talk given by someone who was deeply passionate. Think of the energy you experienced when the musicians were really getting into the music.

As I mentioned earlier, the more I got into the music, the better I played, and the better I played, the more I got into the music. It was a positive feedback loop of enthusiasm that I was generating within myself.

Then I noticed that the longer I remained in flow, the bigger the loop would grow to the point where others would notice and become enthusiastic as well.

> Whether negative or positive, a leader's energy sets the tone for all. Enthusiasm is the energy of positivity. To know your unique Flow Strategy™ is to know how to not only access your enthusiasm, but to exude that enthusiasm in a way that is energetically irresistible to others.

Flow is purpose-based peak performance. We experience purpose in the 40,000 neurons in our heart, not our head[9].

When we're in flow, our energy is exuding three feet all around us. Imagine a three-foot circle around me. All the people within that circle are syncing up to my energy and exuding their own three-foot circles. Now the audience gets looped in and everyone is now connected through a synergistic state of group flow.

9   Alshami, Ali M., "Pain: Is It All in the Brain or the Heart?" (PubMed, 2019 Nov 14;23(12):88), https://pubmed.ncbi.nlm.nih.gov/31728781/.

"... The magnetic fields produced by the heart are involved in energetic communication, which we also refer to as cardio-electromagnetic communication. The heart is the most powerful source of electromagnetic energy in the human body, producing the largest rhythmic electromagnetic field of any of the body's organs. The heart's electrical field is about 60 times greater in amplitude than the electrical activity generated by the brain. This field, measured in the form of an electrocardiogram (ECG), can be detected anywhere on the surface of the body. Furthermore, the magnetic field produced by the heart is more than 100 times greater in strength than the field generated by the brain and can be detected up to three feet away from the body, in all directions, using SQUID-based magnetometers.[10]"

---

10   McCraty, Rollin, *Science of the Heart, Volume 2*. (California: HeartMath, November 2015), https://www.heartmath.org/research/science-of-the-heart/energetic-communication/.

The key here is that the more you develop your relationship with your flow state, the more you connect with your own intrinsic motivation. The more you connect with your own intrinsic motivation, the more amplified the impact on those around you.

"It's you, being you."

Personal side effects of being in flow include:
- Living your values
- Authenticity
- Confidence
- Refueled
- Whole, happy, fulfilled

Leadership side effects of being in flow include:
- Enroll others
- Increase engagement
- Improve morale, motivation, inspiration
- Build trust
- Increase commitment

"Flow is the energy of influence."

Create Flow Culture™

Leading in a state of flow is leading by example. It's the first step toward creating Flow Culture™ whether that involves building a snowman with your family, leading a team of volunteers, or transforming a corporate culture where your people can be in their excellence and feel whole, happy, and fulfilled.

In addition to everything you've already learned about what flow is, Flow Strategy™, and the Universal Entry Point into Flow, you will have to remove flow's biggest killer of flow: disruptions.

"Interruptions are the #1 Killer of Flow".

After a recent speaking engagement, a woman said to me, "It takes me two hours of daily uninterrupted time to do the most important, as well as the most favorite part of my work. All day people ask "quick questions" and it drives me nuts. So, I've been working after hours just to have the peace and quiet to do my work. Now that I know what flow is, combined with defining my Flow Strategy™, I feel empowered to create an interruption-free zone and complete my work during work hours. I also learned how important purpose is in taking our skills and challenges to a new dimension and the fulfillment that brings. It's obvious that a number of my co-workers have lost their spark. I can't wait to help them bring purpose back into the picture."

Here are the steps to expand your leadership into creating a culture that embraces and thrives in flow.

Key Components for Creating Flow Culture™

Flow Education: Educate your people on what flow is.

Flow Strategy™: Coaching for people to discover their unique Flow Strategies™.

Universal Entry Point into Flow: Training on how to implement the Skill-Challenge-Purpose model.

Interruption Management: This will be unique to each organization but can include things like changing policies about all emails having to be responded to within the hour, appointing certain rooms to be quiet zones, company-wide time blocking for individuals to have three hours of uninterrupted time.

TAKEAWAYS

Leadership

Flow is the energy of influence.

Personal Side Effects
- Living your values
- Authenticity
- Confidence
- Refueled
- Whole, happy, fulfilled

Leadership Side Effects
- Enroll others
- Increase engagement
- Improve morale, motivation, inspiration
- Build trust
- Increase commitment

Interruptions

#1 killer of flow

Create Flow Culture™
- Flow education
- Flow Strategy™
- Universal entry point into flow
- Interruption management

QUESTIONS FOR REFLECTION

Observational Learning

- How has observing others influenced your personal and professional development?
- Can you think of specific examples where this has shaped your leadership style?

Embracing Challenges

- Reflect on a time when you faced a significant challenge in your career. How did you overcome it, and what did you learn about yourself in the process?

Leadership in Flow

- How can you apply your Flow Strategy™ to enhance your leadership?
- What steps can you take to lead by example and create a positive feedback loop of enthusiasm in your team?

Energetic Communication

❑ Have you noticed the impact of your energy on those around you?
❑ How can you use this awareness to foster a synergistic state of group flow in your work or community?

Mitigating Interruptions

❑ What are the biggest interruptions you face in your work?
❑ How can you create an interruption-free zone to enhance your productivity and flow?

Creating Flow Culture™

❑ How can you help your team or organization embrace and thrive in a culture based on flow?
❑ What strategies can you implement to remove barriers to flow and increase engagement and fulfillment?

Chapter 6

FLOW IN ACTION

"I'm having a stream-of-consciousness day." That's what my husband, John, and I say to each other when we have a day with nothing scheduled, and our plan is to *go with the flow in order to be in flow.*

To be clear, when my husband and I decide to have a stream-of-consciousness day, we are purposefully choosing to spend the day in our most exalted way.

As professional musicians, we have spent decades experiencing the Key Components for Integrating Flow. We're keenly aware of when we're in flow and when we're not. If spending a day in flow is our ideal, then you have an idea of the degree to which we value being in flow. We're highly educated in flow and have had decades of experience activating it. We've cultivated different flow cultures. For John, an interruption-free environment is a must. For me, an environment filled with feedback and bouncing ideas around is my idea of productive fun. Even on non-stream-of-consciousness days, we prioritize segments of our day to be in flow. For us, a day without flow is a day without sunshine.

You, too, can intentionally integrate flow into your work and life.

Key Components for Integrating Flow into Work and Life

Flow Education: Learn the neuroscience of flow and how it supports you to thrive.

Flow Awareness: Increase your ability to recognize when you're in flow.

Flow Value: Hold the benefits of flow in high regard.

Flow Activation: Utilize practical strategies to enter into a state of flow.

Flow Culture™: Foster environments conducive to flow states.

Flow Prioritization: Identify flow as vitally important for success and fulfillment in work and life.

Flow may be a new idea to you. You may live seamlessly in flow, or you may be anywhere in between. Developing a relationship with your flow state is a journey of self-awareness, self-discovery, and self-actualization beyond what you ever could have imagined for yourself.

Integrating flow into your life can occur during everything from a daily mundane task to a high-stakes event.

Have you ever had a shower moment when ideas and insights were coming from out of the blue? Like flow, when you take a shower your pre-frontal cortex becomes quiet. Without the decision-making machine turned on, your mind is open to receive new thoughts.

But that doesn't happen with every shower. One fun way to see if you can activate a flow-like state is to borrow from the universal entry point of flow at the intersection of skill and challenge. Choose a problem you'd like to solve. Set your intention to work out the challenge during your shower. Then forget about it and go about washing up. If the ideas come in, be prepared to document them before they run down the drain with the water.

Another simple way to activate flow is to take a problem for a walk. Csikszentmihalyi specifies that being out in nature, as well as moving your body, gives you access to flow. Like the shower, take a challenge for a walk, and be prepared to capture any ideas that come your way.

The day I couldn't get into the music was the day I learned I couldn't take flow for granted. This was a high-stakes moment when I hadn't shown up at my best. I had to find a way to get into flow on demand because my reputation and job security were at risk and depended on it. Developing the three-step Flow Strategy™ system was all about defining how I personally get into flow.

*"When you define it,
you own it."*

We all need to learn how to stand in our own power and access flow. For example, let's take public speaking. It's common knowledge that 75 percent of people fear it. That means scenarios like job interviews, small meetings, speaking in front of large groups, or presenting a pitch for funding are all high-stakes, seriously uncomfortable events for most people.

In the heat of the moment, some people can't remember what to say. Others are afraid to jinx it by over-preparing. There are people who don't prepare at all because they just want to speak from the heart. Do any of these sound like they set you up for success?

In each of these cases, you can use the universal entry point of flow as an assessment tool to set you up for success.

Skill

Do you have the skills required for the kind of public speaking you'll be doing? What needs to be improved? Storytelling? Organizing your ideas? Answering unexpected questions? Now you know specifically what skills to hone.

Challenge

Clearly identify the challenges, especially the ones that are the most worrisome. This is different for everyone because challenge is subjective. Aim to minimize as many of the challenges as possible.

Purpose

With regards to what you plan to speak about, feel into the emotions of the meaning and purpose to take things to another dimension.

Remember, if you're over-challenged, flow won't ignite. Being slightly out of your comfort zone is the sweet spot that ignites flow. When it comes to public speaking, just being there in front of other people is oftentimes the right amount of challenge for the magic to happen. That's why it's so important to prepare.

If you have extreme anxiety, I highly recommend hydration, aerobic exercise, and massaging your Achilles tendon daily leading up to your event, with one last time being right before you speak.

When it comes to the moments before your presentation, close your eyes, put your hands on your heart, and remember a time when you've been in your flow state. Imagine your Flow Strategy™ in action. What are you doing on the inside? Why is it so meaningful? This is the energy from which you want to speak.

By now, you may have a different point of view about this statement from Chapter 1.

*"If you can dream it, you can be it.
But if you can experience it,
you can repeat it."*

Here are my last thoughts about jinxing yourself by over preparing, or not preparing at all so you can speak from the heart. What I like about these ideas is that you have an intuitive sense about how a challenge brings out the best in you. A word of caution, however—you'll have to assess your own relationship with risk. For example, I've worked with people who didn't prepare, speaking instead from the heart, and things went south, leaving them feeling humiliated. Some people thrive with a memorized script. Others thrive with a memorized outline. But rarely do people thrive with little to zero preparation.

While these steps are specific to public speaking, they represent ways to integrate all the techniques to get into flow from this how-to manual.

When it comes to retirement, many people can't wait to have time for themselves to do the things they love. In a masterclass, I worked with a group of music students, one of whom was a retiree who had returned to her love of music. As a result of our conversations about using flow to get into the music, she had an epiphany about her working years. "I didn't know there was a name for that!" is a common statement I get when people receive flow education. It was the same with this music student. As you read about her new perspectives, you'll see her checking off all of the boxes of Flow Awareness, Value, Education, Activation, Culture, and Prioritization.

Let me introduce you to Jean Koh Peters.

Yale Law School

JEAN KOH PETERS
Sol Goldman Clinical Professor Emeritus of Law
Yale Law School

January 5, 2022

Dear Diane,

I am so grateful for the Next Level Coaching and two masterclasses you offered us in December. I wanted to share some reflections on the thoughtful resources and exercises on flow that you taught us.

As I mentioned, I taught and supervised students representing refugees seeking asylum and children at risk of foster care at Yale Law School for three decades ending with my retirement in 2019. I realize now that one of my most powerful resources in navigating the unmanageability of the workload and trauma exposure of that work was organizing my time to maximize flow in all my activities: supervising students in regular meetings, actively lawyering with them in court, client work and other proceedings, writing (including two books and several articles), preparing for and teaching classes, administrative meetings, and preparing for and giving professional presentations. Of course, the most challenging period was when my children were at home with me—was this too much of a good life? While I didn't know the term "flow strategy" at that time, I spontaneously problem-solved whenever I found myself experiencing the total blissful absorption in my work and family life and the ability to bear fruit in my tasks almost disproportionately quickly to the time spent. Whether it was a well-timed decaf latte coupled with a John Williams soundtrack to drop me into flow, titrating up and down skill and challenge levels on tasks for me and my students, setting up in front of my fireplace for a long difficult editing session on an asylum brief, or chipping away at a worrisome case problem or book chapter in fellowship with committed, kind, and hard-working students ready for daily work together, I amassed a number of surefire ways to get the work done, happily, joyfully, and with way less wear and tear—which I now identify as flow strategies.

Over the decades, time out of flow became more and more intolerable. When flow failed, I trudged through tasks that took forever, offered no fulfillment, and grated throughout the process. During these periods, my sleep, body, and mental state suffered. At first, I thought this applied only to tasks imposed on me, rather than freely chosen, but I found over time that I could befriend even odious, tedious, or overwhelming tasks with my flow strategies. (Reading administrative files on a deadline goes down a lot smoother with a decaf latte and Princess Leia's theme!)

As I mentioned, I love the definition of vocation from Frederick Buechner—"where your deep gladness and the world's deep hunger meet." It was deeply part of my vocation to help my students to search for their vocations, which often meant plumbing their deep gladness.

I found that my students naturally developed their own flow strategies when they and I seized the moments when flow came and reasoned backward to find out what brought it forth, and then worked those conditions into their work. I urged my students to trust their deep gladness and bring it into their daily routines. Many of my students found flow during and after their favorite sports or exercise, cooking, meditation, journaling/morning pages, creativity, or dialogue with trusted colleagues. As you know, flow is contagious—so many times, when I struggled with distraction or anxiety on my own, my students arriving for a meeting in flow brought me with them back into that timeless, ever-hopeful space.

I hope that I sometimes also helped them out of distraction and worry as well. Law school can be a deeply painful, stressful, aggressive, and self-annihilating place, especially for the many women and students of color whom I was privileged to teach. The high stakes of our work, serving clients who literally struggled to be at home in the world, exiled from all they knew, often began as a paralyzing force for a student with her first client, still unsure about her vocation in the law. Students arrived at my office loaded with their other commitments, barraged by social media, and often terribly distressed by national political forces impinging on our efforts. Their flow strategies helped them to turn to the work, with hope and growing confidence, taking on what was manageable, over and over, until at the end of the semester they found themselves amazed to have gone to trial, written a brief, even won asylum—all things they had never truly believed they could do.

I am so grateful to have your rubrics to think through these issues from my past work life and bring these flow strategies into my retirement. I wish you the very best in your important work in bringing flow strategies into the workplace.

Sincerely,
Jean

TAKEAWAYS

Key Components for Integrating Flow

- **Flow Education:** Learn the neuroscience of flow and how it supports you to thrive.
- **Flow Awareness:** Increase your ability to recognize when you're in flow.
- **Flow Value:** Hold the benefits of flow in high regard.
- **Flow Activation:** Utilize practical strategies to enter into a state of flow.
- **Flow Culture™:** Foster environments conducive to flow states.
- **Flow Prioritization:** Identify flow as vitally important for success and fulfillment in work and life.

Public Speaking

When 75 percent of people fear public speaking, flow can help.

- Apply the universal entry point into flow.
- Utilize your Flow Strategy™.
- Hydrate, exercise, Achilles tendon massage.
- Get into your heart. Close your eyes with your hands on your heart and replay a memory of a time when you were in flow.
- Prepare.

QUESTIONS FOR REFLECTION

Stream of Consciousness

- Have you ever chosen a day to simply go with the flow?
- How did it impact your productivity and well-being?

Flow Culture™

- What kind of environment do you need to foster flow in your work or personal life?
- How can you create or enhance this environment?

Flow in Daily Tasks

- Can you recall a time when you experienced flow during a mundane task?
- What factors contributed to this state, and how can you replicate it?

Activating Flow

- What simple activities, like taking a walk or a shower, help you get into a flow-like state?
- How can you use these activities to solve problems or generate ideas?

Public Speaking and Flow

- How can you use the concept of flow to improve your public speaking or presentations?
- What specific skills and challenges do you need to address?

Applying Flow Strategy™

- When you define it, you own it. What does *owning it* mean to you?

Chapter 7

IN FLOW

Flow or no flow, will life still happen, and challenges come your way? Of course. The question is, how do we navigate through the ups and downs of it all?

With this in mind, I have one more story to share.

I'm 15 years old in my room, blasting the music. Not rock 'n' roll. I'm listening to a violin concerto. In my imagination, it's as if I'm the soloist, standing center stage, pouring the core of my soul into every note I play.

It's like I've discovered what makes me tick.

This memory has been my most vivid flow state vision. But why? Why would I remember that?

In reality, I found myself playing in a lot of orchestras. I did a really good job. Not child prodigy good, but hardworking good. During these real-life experiences, the music would just sweep me away, and I spent hours of uninterrupted time in flow.

But life happens and you quickly learn that interruptions are the #1 killer of flow. Both minor interruptions and big interruptions.

It's now 15 years into my role as the concertmaster. My son is at the height of his teenage rebellion along with being deeply depressed. My mom is contending with Alzheimer's and, by extension, so am I. It's a lot. I don't even realize how much until I'm sitting on stage, performing a Beethoven Symphony, with no emotion. I feel like a piece of cardboard. It's like the part of me that used to make me tick has completely shut down.

During the eight years that I take care of my mom, I think that putting everything that matters to me on the back burner, including flow, is the right thing to do.

My students leave me for other violin teachers. I take a year's leave of absence from the orchestra. A year later, I retire. I sell my entire music collection, my high-precision violin bow, and my gorgeous antique violin, which have been my musical voice for decades.

I'm stuck and I can't see a path back to flow.

Three years later, I'm sitting in a movie theater watching a documentary about a group of counterculture artists. They are questioning everything. Who's to say what art is and what art isn't? Who's to say that this art is valuable, and this art isn't?

That night, I can't sleep. I feel the power of the violin coming back on stage with me. The next morning, I borrow a violin. I play a little Bach. Nope. I play a pop song. YES! As a result of this ten-minute experiment, I find out I'm not done with the violin. I'm done with classical music.

A week later, I borrow an electric violin, and six weeks after that I'm writing my own music and combining the violin with my speaking.

That night when I was sitting on stage feeling empty, distant, and numb, I was so confused.

Later on, I hear about a researcher who discovered that orchestral musicians typically burn out after two decades. Oh! So, I'm a statistic.

But there's one thing I've learned for sure. There's always a path back to flow.

I watched my son work himself out of his depression by following his passion for aviation. Now, as a professional pilot, he's the most motivated, focused, and happiest I've ever seen him.

I remember when my parents used to say "Diane, we just want you to be happy…" As a teen, I'd heave a sigh and roll my eyes. But now as a parent, I get it.

Isn't that what we all want? To be happy? For our family and friends to be happy? For our colleagues and clients to just be happy?

As for me, finding a way to reconnect with the violin was like coming home, but far better than I could have ever imagined.

Yes, you may have small or big interruptions in your life, but whether or not you can see the path, there's always an undercurrent of possibility and a new way to evolve.

I was a guest on a podcast with a colleague of mine named Tyler. Toward the end, Tyler says, "Okay, so clearly, you're not 15 in your room blasting the music anymore. After 28 years you're done teaching violin. You don't even play in an orchestra anymore. But during your keynotes, you do stand center stage. You do pour the core of your soul into every word you speak, and every note you play. From where I sit, it certainly looks like you've become the soloist."

Mind blown. I never saw it. Back when I was all busy dedicating myself to becoming a violinist in an orchestra, I had lost sight of the original dream. But somehow, the original dream never lost sight of me.

That day I learned from Tyler that flow state visions are not unrealistic ideas for you to shut down, brush under the rug, and discredit. They exist for you to see your true genius and your heart's most burning desires.

Now, clearly, I can't promise this idyllic state every minute of every day. What I can promise you is this: when you spend more time in flow, you experience more inspiration and joy in everything you do, and that seed gets planted into all the different landscapes of your life.

When you unlock your flow, on a personal level, it's exhilarating.

But what if you could share your gift with others? When your genius and your heart become one, you can solve problems, help others, and make the changes you want to see in your life and in this world.

Flow is not a mindset. It's a mind state. Utilizing your Flow Strategy™ generates the mindset that gets you into that mind state.

It's not about learning a different way to think. It's about learning to think differently about being in your natural state of flow.

Every one of us is wired for this. Discovering your Flow Strategy™ will give you the gift to shift, so you can get into your life, like a musician gets into the music, on cue.

ABOUT THE AUTHOR

International speaker and violinist Diane Allen is a TEDx/TED speaker, and thought leader who speaks on increasing the meaning, joy, and fulfillment in one's work and life by accessing the flow state. Years before neuroscientists discovered the positive impact the flow state has on achieving peak performance, Diane had already experienced the power of flow in her own career as a violinist. It was her unique approach to getting into flow, on demand, that landed her a spot on the TEDxNaperville stage as well as features on TED, ABC, CBS, NBC, FOX, Associated Press, *Boston Herald, Authority Magazine,* and *Thrive Global.* Diane was the concertmaster of the Central Oregon

Symphony for 15 years, a beloved violin teacher for 28 years, and author of the *Fingerboard Workbook* series for violin, viola, cello, and bass.

Diane is extremely proud of her husband, John, who is also a musician, and her son Scott, who is a pilot. Both exemplify what it's like to live a meaningful life at the intersection of flow, passion, and purpose.

Today, the author of *Flow: Unlock Your Genius, Love What You Do* is known for her experiential keynotes, training, and coaching programs that go Beyond Engagement™ featuring her three-step Flow Strategy™ system which empowers people to get into their flow state, be in their genius, and love what they do.

Website: dianeallen.com

TEDx Talk: ted.com/talks/diane_allen_how_to_find_flow_and_lose_yourself_in_it

Album: *Finding Flow*

LinkedIn: @dianeallenspeaker
Facebook: @dianeallenspeaker
Instagram: @dianeallenspeaker
X: @dianeaspeaker